The month of May, from the illuminated manuscript
Les Très Riches Heures du duc de Berry

The Story of a Special Day
Volume 145

May
24

144th day of the year
(145th in leap years)
221 days remaining
until the end of the year.

by Michael Dobson

Timespinner
Press

Table of Contents

Cover: "The Great East River Suspension Bridge,"(Brooklyn Bridge), by Currier & Ives — for the *Event of the Day.*

Back Cover and Frontispiece: The month of May, from the French Gothic illuminated manuscript *Les Très Riches Heures du duc de Berry.*

May 24 Quotations

"He who rejects change is the architect of decay. The only human institution which rejects progress is the cemetery."

— Harold Wilson, died May 24, 1995

"There are simply two kinds of music, good music and the other kind."

— Duke Ellington, died May 24, 1974

"Yesterday's just a memory; tomorrow's never what it's supposed to be."

— Bob Dylan, born May 24, 1941

"The surest defense against Evil is extreme individualism, originality of thinking, whimsicality, even — if you will — eccentricity."

— Joseph Brodsky, born May 24, 1940

"Affairs go on, and all will take some shape or other, but it keeps one in hot water all the time."

— Queen Victoria, born May 24, 1819

"No, liberty is not made for us: we are too ignorant, too vain, too presumptious, too cowardly, too vile, too corrupt too attached to rest and to pleasure, too much slaves to fortune to ever know the true price of liberty."

— Jean-Paul Marat, born May 24, 1743

Event of the Day
The Brooklyn Bridge Opens

The Brooklyn Bridge by Currier & Ives, 1883

"If you believe that, I've got a bridge to sell you." New York's Brooklyn Bridge, a world-famous icon of New York City, was the world's longest suspension bridge when it opened to the public on May 24, 1883.

The Brooklyn Bridge spans the East River, connecting the boroughs of Manhattan and Brooklyn. Its main span is just under 1,600 feet (490 meters) long, with a total length of over a mile from end to end.

Towering nearly 300 feet (85 meters) above the water, it has been named one of the "Seven Wonders of the Industrial World," and is both a National Historic Landmark and a National Historic Civil Engineering Landmark.

The bridge was designed by a German immigrant, John Augustus Roebling, who died from an injury sustained while conducting surveys for the new bridge. Responsibility passed to his son, Washington Roebling, who led the project for the rest of the 13-year construction. Washington Roebling was paralyzed as a result of what was then known as "caisson disease," and managed much of the work through his wife Emily.

(A caisson is a metal structure placed on the riverbed and pumped out with compressed air so that workers could operate underwater. The difference in air pressure results in decompression sickness when people move too rapidly from one environment to another, just as happens to deep sea divers, where the condition is known as "the bends.)

The bridge cost $15.5 million to build (at least $400 million today), and claimed 27 lives. Many workers also became permanently disabled by caisson disease.

The Brooklyn Bridge opened on May 24, 1883, to great fanfare. Thousands of people attended the opening ceremony, which was headlined by US President Chester A. Arthur and New York City Mayor Franklin Edison, who crossed the bridge to meet Brooklyn Mayor Seth Low. (Roebling was unable to attend, but held a banquet at his house.)

Ships crowded the East Bay, cannons were fired, and a fireworks display lit up the night sky. During that first day, 1,800 vehicles and over 150,000 people crossed over between Manhattan and Brooklyn.

While the bridge is no longer used for horse carriages and trolley cars, it carries motor vehicles on six lanes, with a center walkway for pedetrians and bicycles. Trucks and buses are prohibited because of the roadway's low height and weight restrictions. It has managed to keep up with much heavier vehicles than originally intended, because the bridge was designed many times stronger than necessary. It remains standing while many contemporary bridges are long gone.

Besides jokes about "selling the Brooklyn Bridge," the bridge has been involved in many stories.

As with most public works projects, a number of properties were displaced for the bridge. One of them, the Osgood House, served as the first Presidential Mansion during a two-year period in which New York City was the national capital. George Washington lived there from 1789 to 1790, and a plaque marks the spot.

A "Brodie," slang for a suicidal leap, comes from the Brooklyn Bridge. It is named for Steve Brodie, who claimed to have jumped from the bridge and survived, though the incident is still disputed. Many other jumpers were not so fortunate.

In 1919, Giorgio Pessi, a World War I fighter ace from Italy, flew what was then the world's largest airplane, the Caproni Ca.5, under the bridge. In 1993,

Thierry Devaux performed eight illegal bungee jumps from the bridge. The bridge has been the site of terrorist attacks, including the 1994 shooting by Rashid Baz of a van filled with Orthodox Jews, and a 2003 al-Qaeda plot to cut through the bridge's support wires with a blowtorch.

The Brooklyn Bridge was the central metaphor in poet Hart Crane's *The Bridge*. It has appeared in such films as *It Happened in Brooklyn, I Am Legend, The Dark Night Rises*, and *The Avengers*. Its construction was chronicled in the 1981 Ken Burns miniseries *Brooklyn Bridge*.

While many other bridges today connect the island of Manhattan with Long Island and the mainland of the United States, the Brooklyn Bridge remains the most famous and one of the most beautiful today.

The Brooklyn Bridge in 2011, taken from the Brooklyn side showing downtown Manhattan in the background. (Photo: Hakilon)

May 24 Holidays and Celebrations

Aldersgate Day (Methodism)

Aldersgate Day is celebrated by Methodists to commemorate the "confirmation of his salvation by the grace of God" of John Wesley, founder of the Methodist movement, on May 24, 1738, in a meeting room in Aldersgate Street, London.

Battle of Pichincha Day (Ecuador)

The Battle of Pichincha, which took place May 24, 1822, near the city of Quito, achieved the independence of the provinces that would later form the Republic of Ecuador. May 24 is celebrated as a public holiday in Ecuador to commemorate that victory, and serves as Ecuador's Independence Day.

Bermuda Day (Bermuda)

The public holiday of Bermuda Day is celebrated on May 24, or on the nearest weekday if May 24 falls on a weekend. It marks the traditional first day that residents will go into the sea following winter, and the first day Bermuda shorts can be worn as business attire. A parade and a road race are part of the festivities.

Commonwealth Day (Belize)

The Central American nation of Belize, part of the Commonwealth of Nations, celebrates Commonwealth Day as a public holiday on May 24. It is officially celebrated as the Queen's birthday (although Elizabeth II was born on April 21). Celebrations include horse races, cycle races, and a three day Chocolate Festival.

Independence Day (Eritrea)

May 24 in the African nation of Eritrea celebrates that country's independence from Ethiopia in 1993.

Lubiri Memorial Day (Buganda)

Buganda, a kingdom within the African nation of Uganda, commemorates the destruction of the royal compound (Lubiri Palace) in the May 1966 Battle of Mengo Hill, resulting in the theft and destruction of historical and religious artifacts, including the sacred *Mujaguzo* drums.

Saints Cyril and Methodius Day (Eastern Orthodox Church)

In Eastern Orthodox Christianity, Saints Cyril and Methodius are credited with bringing Christianity to the Slavic nations, and are venerated not merely as saints but with the additional title of "equal-to-apostles" (ἰσαπόστολος). May 24 is celebrated in numerous nations as Saints Cyril and Methodius Day.

Icon of Saints Cyril and Methodius

In Bulgaria, it is known as "Bulgarian Education and Culture, and Slavonic Literature Day" (Ден на българската просвета и култура и на славянската писменост), a public holiday.

In the Republic of Macedonia, it is the "Saints Cyril and Methodius, Slavonic Enlighteners'

Day" (Св. Кирил и Методиј, Ден на словенските просветители), a national holiday.

In Russia, it is "Slavonic Literature and Culture Day (День славянской письменности и культуры), celebrated unofficially but not a public holiday.

The Czech Republic and Slovakia celebrate the event on July 5. The Eastern Orthodox Church feast day for the saints is May 11; Roman Catholics and Anglicans (Episcopalians) celebrated February 14; and Lutherans vary, with some using May 11 and others February 14.

Christian Feast Days

In **Western Christianity**, May 24 is the feast day of Sara, Vincent of Lérins (also in Eastern Orthodox Christianity), and David I of Scotland.

In **Eastern Orthodox Christianity**, May 24 is the feast of Symeon Stylites the Younger of Wonderful Mountain, Saint Kyriakos the Wonderworker, Nun-martyr Martha of Monemvasia, Saint Patrice, Saint Elpidios, and the Glorification of Saint Xenia of Petersburg, fool-for-Christ. (These events are observed on June 6 by "Old Calendarists.")

What Happened on May 24?

1607 CE – **First English Settlers at Jamestown**

On May 24, 1607 (O.S. May 14, see page XX), the ships Susan Constant, Discovery, and Godspeed, carrying 104 English settlers, reached Jamestown Island and established a new colony, originally named "James His Towne" and later "Jamestown" in honor of King James VI and I, the current monarch of England. Jamestown served as the capital of Virginia until 1699, when it was moved to the town of Williamsburg.

1798 CE – **Irish Rebellion Begins**

On May 24, 1798, the United Irishman Rebellion (*Éirí Amach na nÉireannach Aontaithe*) against British rule in Ireland began. The first battle of the rebellion began just after dawn on May 24 around Dublin and quickly spread. Although the rebels enjoyed some early successes, British forces eventually prevailed, committing numerous atrocities, matched in a few cases by the rebels themselves. French reinforcements did not change the outcome. By October the rebellion was over, with estimates of the death toll ranging from 10,000 to 50,000.

1830 CE – *Mary Had a Little Lamb* Published

The nursery rhyme "Mary Had a Little Lamb," written by Sara Josepha Hale, was first published by Marsh, Capen & Lyon of Boston on May 24, 1830. It was based on an actual incident, when Mary Sawyer took her pet lamb to Redstone School in the town of Sterling, Massachusettts. A statue of Mary's little lamb is in the town center of Sterling and the Redstone School was purchased by Henry Ford and moved to Sudbury, Massachusetts. The rhyme also has the distinction of being the first thing recorded by Thomas Edison's phonograph in 1877. The rhyme was set to music a few years later by Lowell Mason.

Redstone School (Photo: Dudesleeper)

1830 CE – **First Common Carrier Railroad in the United States**

Although the Baltimore & Ohio (B&O) Railroad was not the first American railroad, it was the first "common carrier," offering scheduled freight and passenger service to the public. It began scheduled service from downtown Baltimore to the town of Ellicott's Mills (today known as Ellicott City) in Maryland, a distance of 13 miles. The Ellicott City Station, the oldest surviving railroad station in America, is currently a museum.

Ellicott City B&O Railroad Station, oldest surviving railroad station in the United States

1844 CE – **Samuel Morse's Telegraph Opens**

Samuel Morse, pioneer of the telegraph and creator of Morse code, developed the concept of the telegraph in 1832 and demonstrated it publicly for the first time in 1838. The first telegraph line, funded by the Federal government, stretched from Washington, DC, to Baltimore, a distance of 38 miles, and opened officially on May 24, 1844, with Samuel Morse sending the famous message, "What hath God wrought," from the U.S. Capitol to the B&O Mount Clare Station in Baltimore.

Samuel F. B. Morse (Photo: Mathew Brady)

1856 CE – **Pottawatomie Massacre**

On the night of May 24, 1856, in response to the sacking of Lawrence, Kansas, by pro-slavery forces, John Brown and his band killed five settlers near Pottawatomie Creek, Kansas.

1935 CE – **First Night Baseball Game**

The first night game in Major League Baseball history took place on May 24, 1935, with the Cincinnati Reds beating the Philadelphia Phillies 2-1 at Crosley Field. (Night games had taken place in the Negro League and the minor leagues as early as the late 1920s.)

1962 CE – **Flight of Aurora 7**

On May 24, 1962, Project Mercury launched its second manned space mission: Mercury-Atlas 7. Astronaut Scott Carpenter rode the Aurora 7 space capsule through three Earth orbits in just under five hours. A targeting problem resulted in the spacecraft splashing down about 250 miles off course. The Aurora 7 is now in Chicago's Museum of Science and Industry.

1970 CE – **World's Deepest Hole**

On May 24, 1970, the Soviet Union began drilling the Kola Superdeep Borehole (Кольская сверхглубокая скважина), a scientific project to drill as deep as possible into the Earth's crust, reaching a depth of 12, 262 meters (40,230 feet), or more than 7-1/2 miles. The project ended in 2005 because of lack of funding.

Launch of Aurora 7

1991 CE – **Operation Solomon**

On May 24, 1991, the Israeli military launched
Operation Solomon (מִבְצָע שלמה), an airlift of
Ethiopian Jews to Israel. Over 36 hours, nonstop
flights of 34 aircraft evacuated 14,325 people. The
seats were taken out of the planes to maximize
carrying capacity. One flight, an El Al 747, set a
world record for single-flight passenger loading,
carrying 1,122 people. Seven pregnant women gave
birth on the planes.

Who Was Born on May 24?

Art and Design

Carmine Infantino (May 24, 1925 — April 4, 2013)

Comic book artist and editor shaped the Silver Age of Comic Books as editorial director and later publisher of DC Comics. He created the look for the modern Flash, developed the "new look" Batman, and made numerous other contributions. He was named to the Comic Book Hall of Fame in 2000.

Peter Ellenshaw (May 24, 1913 — February 12, 2007)

Matte designer and special effects creator Peter Ellenshaw created visual effects and art for numerous films, primarily for Walt Disney, including *Treasure Island* and *Mary Poppins,* winning an Academy Award for the latter.

Emanuel Leutze (May 24, 1816 — July 18, 1868)

German-American painter Emanuel Leutze is best known for his work *Washington Crossing the Delaware.*

Washington Crossing the Delaware, by Emanuel Leutze

Business and Technology

Priscilla Presley (May 24, 1945 —)

Ex-wife of Elvis Presley, actress and business executive Priscilla Presley was chair of Elvis Presley Enterprises and developed Graceland as a major tourist attraction. She also starred in the *Naked Gun* movie series and played Jenna on *Dallas.*

S. I. Newhouse, Sr. (May 24, 1895 — August 29, 1979)

Broadcaster and publisher S. I. Newhouse founded Advance Publications, which grew into a publishing conglomerate that include Condé Nast, Parade, over 30 newspapers, and many other media properties. He accumulated a fortune estimated at $1.5 billion at the time of his death, nearly $5 billion today.

H. B. Reese (May 24, 1878 — May 16, 1956)

American inventor H. B. Reese founded the H. B. Reese Candy Company and created its signature product, Reese's Peanut Butter Cups (below).

Lillian Moller Gilbreth (May 24, 1878 — January 2, 1972)

Psychologist and industrial engineer Lillian Gilbreth is considered the first true organizational psychologist. She and her husband, Frank Gilbreth Sr., also an efficiency expert, had twelve children. The story of their family life makes up the books *Cheaper by the Dozen* and *Belles on their Toes*, written by their children. Both books were made into films.

Charlie Taylor (May 24, 1868 — January 30, 1956)

Mechanic Charlie Taylor built the first aircraft engine used by the Wright brothers and helped build and maintain the early Wright airplanes.

Film and Television

Jo Joyner (May 24, 1978 —)

Joyner played Tanya Branning in the long running BBC soap opera *EastEnders*.

Will Sasso (May 24, 1975 —)

Sasso was a cast member on *MADtv* and played Curly in the 2012 film *The Three Stooges.*

Eric Close (May 24, 1967 —)

Eric Close had major roles in the TV series *Without a Trace* and *Nashville*.

Dana Ashbrook (May 24, 1967 —)

Ashbrook is known for playing Bobby Briggs on the TV series *Twin Peaks* and its associated film.

Shinichirō Watanabe (渡辺 信一郎) (May 24, 1965 —)

Anime director Watanabe is known for the anime series *Cowboy Bebop.*

John C. Reilly (May 24, 1965 —)

Actor John C. Riley was nominated for a Supporting Actor Oscar for his role in *Chicago,* and has appeared in more than 50 films.

Gene Anthony Ray (May 24, 1962 — November 14, 2003)

Dancer and choreographer Ray played Leroy Johnson in the 1980 film *Fame* and its spinoff television series.

Kristin Scott Thomas (May 24, 1960 —)

Kristin Scott Thomas appeared in such films as *Four Weddings and a Funeral* and *The English Patient,* receiving an Academy Award nomination for Best Supporting Actress.

Alfred Molina (May 24, 1953 —)

British actor Alfred Molina had roles in such films as *Raiders of the Lost Ark, Spider-Man 2, Maverick, Not Without My Daughter, Chocolat, The DaVinci Code,* and many more.

Nell Campbell (May 24, 1953 —)

"Little" Nell Campbell is best known for her role in the play *The Rocky Horror Show* and its film version, *The Rocky Horror Picture Show*.

Sybil Danning (May 24, 1952 —)

B movie and cult film actress Sybil Danning appeared in the 1973 film version of *The Three Musketeers*, and had featured roles in such films as *Battle Beyond the Stars, Chained Heat, Reform School Girls*, and *Amazon Women on the Moon*. She appeared twice in *Playboy* magazine.

Jim Broadbent (May 24, 1949 —)

Jim Broadbent won an Academy Award for 2001's *Iris*, and appeared in *Moulin Rouge!, Bridget Jones' Diary*, and *The Iron Lady*. He was Horace Slughorn in the later *Harry Potter* films.

Gary Burghoff (May 24, 1943 —)

Gary Burghoff is most famous for playing "Radar" O'Reilly (right, with McLean Stephenson) in the movie and television series *M*A*S*H*, and is also known for playing the title role in the 1967 off-Broadway musical *You're A Good Man, Charlie Brown*. Earlier in his career, he was the drummer for a band called The Relatives, whose lead singer was Lynda "Wonder Woman" Carter.

Tommy Chong (May 24, 1938 —)

Comedian Tommy Chong is best known as half of the marijuana-themed comedy duo Cheech & Chong.

Michael Lonsdale (May 24, 1931 —)

French actor Michael Lonsdale is known to English-speaking audiences as Sir Hugo Drax in the James Bond film *Moonraker,* Lebel in *The Day of the Jackal,* and M. d'Ivry in *The Remains of the Day.*

Mai Zetterling (May 24, 1925 — March 17, 1994)

Zetterling starred in a number of English films with such actors as Tyrone Power, Richard Widmark, Peter Sellars, and Richard Attenborough, and became a noted Swedish director starting with her 1964 film *Älskande par,* which critic Kenneth Tynan called "one of the most ambitious debuts since *Citizen Kane.*"

Lilli Palmer (May 24, 1914 — January 27, 1986)

German actress Lilli Palmer appeared in such films as *The Story of Anastasia, Mrs. Warren's Profession, The Pleasure of His Company, The Amorous Adventures of Moll Flanders, The Boys from Brazil,* and *The Holcroft Covenant.* She was married to Rex Harrison from 1943 to 1957, and appeared with him in the Broadway hit *Bell, Book and Candle.*

Literature

Mo Willems (May 24, 1968 —)

Children's book author and illustrator Mo Williams won the Theodor Seuss Geisel Medal for his *Elephant and Piggie* books.

Michael Chabon (May 24, 1963 —)

Novelist Michael Chabon's critically acclaimed best-selling works include the Pulitzer winning *The Amazing Adventure of Kavalier & Clay*, the Hugo and Nebula winning *The Yiddish Policemen's Union*, and others.

Joseph Brodsky (Иосиф Бродский) (May 24, 1940 — January 28, 1996)

Russian poet Joseph Brodsky was expelled from the Soviet Union in 1972 and settled in America. He received the 1987 Nobel Prize in Literature and became the United States Poet Laureate in 1991.

Mikhail Sholokhov (Михаил Шолохов) (May 24 [O.S. May 11], 1905 — February 21, 1984)

Internationally known as the author of *And Quiet Flows the Don*, Russian novelist Mikhail Sholokhov won the 1965 Nobel Prize in Literature.

Music

Tommy Page (May 24, 1970 —)

Page had a 1990 Hot 100 #1 hit with "I'll Be Your Everything."

Rosanne Cash (May 24, 1955 —)

Singer-songwriter Rosanne Cash is the daughter of Johnny Cash. She received a Grammy in 1985 for "I Don't Know Why You Don't Want Me," and has been nominated an additional nine times. She has had 11 #1 country hit singles and two gold records.

Patti LaBelle (May 24, 1944 —)

Grammy-winning artist Patti LaBelle's hits include "Lady Marmelade," "If Only You Knew," and "New Attitude." She has been named to the Grammy Hall of Fame, the Hollywood Walk of Fame, the Apollo Hall of Fame, and the Songwriters' Hall of Fame.

Bob Dylan (May 24, 1941 —)

Legendary American singer-songwriter Bob Dylan is considered one of the most influential figures of the 20th century. His 50-year recording career contains such hits as "Blowin' in the Wind," "Highway 61 Revisited," "All Along the Watchtower," and many others. He has received 11 Grammys, an Academy Award, a Golden Globe, and the Presidential Medal of Freedom, and is in the Rock and Roll Hall of Fame, the Nashville Songwriters Hall of Fame, and the Songwriters Hall of Fame.

Bob Dylan at the 1963 Civil Rights March on Washington

Roger Peterson (May 24, 1937 — February 3, 1959)

21-year old pilot Roger Peterson was at the controls of the aircraft crash on February 3, 1959 "The Day the Music Died," in which Buddy Holly, Ritchie Valens, and The Big Bopper also perished.

Politics and Military

Monica Lin Brown (May 24, 1988 —)

US Army medic Monica Lin Brown received the Silver Star in 2007 for heroism under fire. She was the first woman in Afghanistan and only the second woman since World War II to receive the medal.

Jane Byrne (May 24, 1934 —)

Jane Byrne was mayor of Chicago from 1979 to 1983, heading the largest American city with a female mayor.

Wilbur Mills (May 24, 1909 — May 2, 1992)

Democratic congressman from Arkansas, Wilbur Mills chaired the House Ways and Means Committee for seventeen years, holding the post longer than any other person in history. He became known as the "most powerful man in Washington" during his tenure.

Jan Smuts (May 24, 1870 — September 11, 1950)

South African Prime Minister Jan Smuts served as a British field marshal, helped establish the British Commonwealth, designed the League of Nations, and wrote the preamble to the United Nations Charter.

Benjamin Cardozo (May 24, 1870 — July 9, 1938)

Benjamin Cardozo was an associate justice of the Supreme Court from 1932 to his death in 1938.

Queen Victoria (May 24, 1819 — January 22, 1901)

Monarch of the United Kingdom of Great Britain and Ireland and Empress of India, Queen Victoria had the longest reign of any English monarch and the longest of any female monarch in history: 63 years and seven months. She was the last British monarch from the House of Hanover. She succeeded William IV and was in turn succeeded by Edward VII.

Queen Victoria of the United Kingdom (Photo: Alexander Bassano)

Jean-Paul Marat (May 24, 1743 — July 13, 1793)

Journalist and physician Jean-Paul Marat was known as a radical defender of the sans-culottes of the French Revolution. He was assassinated in his bathtub by Charlotte Corday. The Tony Award-winning play *Marat/Sade,* adapted into a 1967 film, is about his death.

Germanicus (May 24, 15 BCE — October 10, 19 CE)

Germanicus Julius Caesar (left, on a gold coin) was a prominent Roman general of the early Empire. He was a member of the Julio-Claudian dynasty: his great uncle was Caesar Augustus, his brother was the future emperor Claudius, his son the emperor Caligula, and his grandson the emperor Nero. Known as a brilliant general, Germanicus himself was considered a potential successor to Augustus, though that honor went instead to Tiberius. He commanded legions on the German frontier, turned several Asian kingdoms into Roman provinces, and died from a mysterious illness, thought by many to have been poison.

Religion

William F. Albright (May 24, 1891 — Septeber 19, 1971)

American archeologist and biblical scholar William Albright founded the Biblical archeology movement.

Abraham Geiger (May 24, 1810 — October 23, 1874)

German rabbi and scholar Abraham Geiger led the founding of Reform Judaism.

Science

Daniel Fahrenheit (May 24, 1686 — September 16, 1736)

Danzig (Gdansk)-born Dutch physicist, engineer, and glassblower Daniel Gabriel Fahrenheit invented the mercury-in-glass thermometer and developed the temperature scale named for him.

William Gilbert (May 24, 1544 — November 30, 1603)

Astronomer William Gilbert is regarded as the father of electrical engineering, electricity, and magnetism. The unit of magnetomotive force, the *gilbert,* is named for him.

Sports

Frank Mir (May 24, 1979 —)

Mixed martial artist Frank Mir was a two-time UFC Heavyweight Champion.

Tracy McGrady (May 24, 1979 —)

Shooting guard Tracy McGrady was ranked #75 on *SLAM Magazine*'s "Top 75 Players of All-Time" in 2003.

Marc Gagnon (May 24, 1975 —)

French Canadian speed skater Marc Gagnon won three gold medals in the 1998 and 2002 Olympic Games.

Kris Draper (May 24, 1971 —)

Detroit Red Wings star Kris Draper won the Stanley Cup four times. He was part of the Detroit "Grind Line."

Ricky Craven (May 24, 1966 —)

ESPN race analyst and former NASCAR driver Ricky Craven won the closest finish in NASCAR Sprint Cup Series history.

Pat Verbeek (May 24, 1964 —)

Ice hockey right wing Pat Verbeek was nicknamed "the Little Ball of Hate." In his career, he achieved over 500 goals and 2,500 penalty minutes.

Joe Dumars III (May 24, 1963 —)

NBA shooting and point guard Joe Dumars was inducted into the Basketball Hall of Fame in 2006.

Héctor Camacho (May 24, 1962 — November 24, 2013)

Boxer Héctor Camacho was WBC Super Featherweight Champion, WBC Lightweight Champion, and WBO Light Welterweight Champion, fighting 88 bouts, winning 79, losing six, and drawing three.

Pelle Lindbergh (May 24, 1959 — November 11, 1985)

Ice hockey goaltender Lindbergh was part of the Swedish national team at the 1980 Lake Placid Olympics and went on to a professional career with the NHL Philadelphia Flyers.

Irena Szewińska (May 24, 1946 —)

Polish sprinter Irena Szewińska won three gold, two silver, and two bronze Olympic medals in five Olympic games from 1964 to 1972. She broke six world records and is the only athlete to have achieve world records in the 100m, 200m, and 400m events.

Lionel Conacher as a football player

Lionel Conacher (May 24, 1902— May 26, 1954)

Canadian athlete and politician Lionel "Big Train" Conacher" played professional football for the Canadian Football League, baseball for the Toronto Maple Leafs, and hockey for the Chicago Black Hawks and the Montreal Maroons. He was named Canada's Greatest Male Athlete of the Half-Century, and named to the Canadian Sports Hall of Fame, the Canadian Football Hall of Fame, the Canadian Lacrosse Hall of Fame, and the Hockey Hall of Fame. Following his athletic career, he served as a member of the Canadian parliament.

Suzanne Lenglen (May 24, 1899 — July 4, 1938)

French tennis player Suzanne Lenglen won 31 championship titles between 1914 and 1926, becoming the first female tennis celebrity. She was nicknamed *La Divine* by the French press.

Robert Garrett (May 24, 1875 — April 25, 1961)

American athlete Robert Garrett won gold medals in the 1896 Olympics in shot put and discus throwing, silver medals in the high jump and long jump, and bronze medals in the 1900 Olympics for shot put and standing triple jump.

Who Died on May 24?

Architecture

Alexey Viktorovich Shchusev (Алексе́й Ви́кторович Щу́сев) (December 10, 1805 — May 24, 1879)

Soviet Russian architect Shchusev's notable works include Moscow's Kazan Railway Station and the Tomb of Lenin. The national museum of Russian architecture is named for him.

Lenin's Tomb

Business

Raymond V. Haysbert (January 19, 1920 — May 24, 2010)

African-American business executive Raymond Haysbert served with the Tuskegee Airmen in World War II, and subsequently worked his way to become CEO of Parks Sausage Company, one of the largest African-American owned US businesses. He was active in civil rights causes and chaired the Greater Baltimore Urban League.

Film and Television

Dick Martin (January 30, 1922 — May 24, 2008)

Comic Dick Martin and his partner Dan Rowan were best known as the co-hosts of the TV sketch comedy series *Rowan & Martin's Laugh-In* from 1968 to 1973.

(Left to right) Tiny Tim, and Dick Martin from *Rowan & Martin's Laugh-In*, 1971

Henry Bumstead (March 17, 1915 — May 24, 2006)

Prolific art director and production designer Henry Bumstead won Academy Awards for *To Kill a Mockingbird* and *The Sting*, and was nominated for *Vertigo* and *Unforgiven*.

Rachel Kempson (May 28, 1910— May 24, 2003)

English actress Rachel Kempson appeared in such films as *Tom Jones, Georgy Girl*, and *Out of Africa*. She is perhaps best known as the wife of actor Sir Michael Redgrave and the mother of actresses Vanessa and Lynn Redgrave.

Edward Mulhare (April 8, 1923 — May 24, 1997)

Irish actor Edward Mulhare appeared in numerous film, television, and stage roles in a career spanning some forty years. He is best remembered as the ghost in the TV series *The Ghost & Mrs. Muir* and as Devon Miles in the 1980s TV series *Knight Rider*.

Literature

Amado Nervo (August 27, 1870 — May 24, 1919)

Amado Nervo is one of the most important poets of 19th century Mexico, and also served his country as an ambassador to Argentina and Uruguay.

Military

Archibald Wavell (May 5, 1883 — May 24, 1950)

British Field Marshall Archibald Wavell, 1st Earl Wavell, was Commander-in-Chief, Middle East, at the beginning of World War II, and subsequently served as Commander-in-Chief, India, and later Viceroy of India until his retirement in 1947.

Music

Duke Ellington (April 29, 1899 — May 24, 1974)

Known as a major figure in the development of jazz, Edward Kennedy "Duke" Ellington's career covered blues, gospel, and classical genres. Among his many hits are "Mood Indigo," "It Don't Mean a Thing (If It Ain't Got That Swing," "Stormy Weather," "Caravan," "Don't Get Around Much Any More," and "Take the A Train." His many honors include the Presidential Medal of Freedom, the Grammy Lifetime Achievement Award, the French Legion of Honor, the Pulitzer Prize, a stamp, and even a US quarter.

Duke Ellington (Photo: Gordon Parks)

Elmore James (January 27, 1918 — May 24, 1963)

Blues guitarist Elmore James was known as the "King of the Slide Guitar." His hits include "The Sky is Crying," "My Bleeding Heart" (famously covered by Jimi Hendrix), and "Shake Your Moneymaker."

Politics and Journalism

Harold Wilson (March 11, 1916 — May 24, 1995)

Labor Party leader Harold Wilson was Prime Minister of the United Kingdom from 1964 to 1970, and again from 1974 to 1976.

Harold Wilson
(Photo: Alan Warren)

John Foster Dulles (February 25, 1888 — May 24, 1959)

American diplomat John Foster Dulles was a leading figure in the development of the United Nations and helped shape American Cold War policy as Secretary of State under US President Dwight D. Eisenhower. Washington's Dulles International Airport is named for him.

William Lloyd Garrison (December 10, 1805 — May 24, 1879)

American abolitionist and journalist William Lloyd Garrison was a founder of the American Anti-Slavery Society and edited the abolitionist newspaper *The Liberator*. After the abolition of slavery in the United States, Garrison was an advocate for temperance and women's suffrage.

Portrait of William Lloyd Garrison by Nathaniel Jocelyn, 1833

Science

Nicolaus Copernicus (February 19, 1473 — May 24, 1543)

Astronomer and mathematician Nicolaus Copernicus triggered the Copernican Revolution with his model that placed the Sun, rather than the Earth, in the center of the solar system. The polymath Copernicus was also a physician, a translator, a diplomat, and an economist whose economic concepts are used to the present day.

Nicolaus Copernicus

Sports

Lou Watson (August 31, 1924 — May 24, 2012)

Watson was head basketball coach for Indiana University from 1966 to 1971.

Morrie Martin (September 3, 1922 — May 24, 2010)

Left-handed MLB pitcher Morrie Martin appeared in 250 games from 1949 to 1959. He was a member of the Army Corps of Engineers in World War II, involved in Operations Torch, Overlord, and Cobra, as well as the Battle of the Bulge.

Vince McMahon, Sr. (July 6, 1914 — May 24, 1984)

Vince McMahon Sr. is best known for founding the World Wide Wrestling Federation (WWE).

Old Tom Morris (June 16, 1821 — May 24, 1908)

Scotsman Tom Morris Sr. is known as a pioneer of professional golf. His son, Tom Morris Jr. (known as "Young Tom Morris") became the first young prodigy in golf history, winning four Open Championship titles before the age of 21. Both father and son are in the World Golf Hall of Fame.

Old Tom Morris (left) with son Young Tom Morris
(Photo: Thomas Rodger)

May
The Fifth Month

"Then came fair May, the fairest maid on ground,
Deck'd all with dainties of the season's pride,
And throwing flowers out of her lap around. ."

— *Edward Spenser,* The Faerie Queene, *Book VII*

According to many scholars, the month of May takes its name from the Roman goddess Maia, an earth goddess who was the mother of Mercury. The poet Ovid, on the other hand, claimed that May took its name from the Latin *maiores*, meaning ancestors. In either case, the month of May in ancient Rome was marked by sacrifices to Maia, and her son Mercury was honored on the Ides of May (May 15).

May is the fifth month of the year in both Julian and Gregorian calendars. It was originally the third month in ancient Rome, because the new year began on March 1. Although Julius Caesar changed the length of several months during his great calendar reform (the Julian calendar), the length of May has remained constant at 31 days.

In the northern hemisphere, May occurs in the springtime, and in the southern hemisphere, May takes place in fall. Strangely, no other month begins or ends on the same day of the week as the beginning or ending of May, although January of the following year always begins and ends on the same day of the week as this year's May.

May in Other Cultures

In Latin and Old English, the month of May was named *Maius*, and it is *Mai* in French. In Arabic, the month is مايو, pronounced *māyū*. In Chinese, the equivalent month is 五月. Croatians call the month *svibanj* and in Czech it is *květen*. In Finland, it is *toukokuu*. The Jewish month of Sivan (סִיוָן) normally falls in May-June. It is the third month of the Jewish ecclesiastical year. The Irish called the month *bealtaine*, and it marked the beginning of summer. Slovenians call May *veliki traven*, or the month of the big grass.

May Superstitions

- May is an unlucky month for getting married.

- Never buy a broom in May.

- "Wash a blanket in May / Wash a dear one away."

- Cats born in May will bring snakes into the house.

- "Those who bathe in May / Will soon be laid in clay."

May Symbols

Birthstone: Emerald

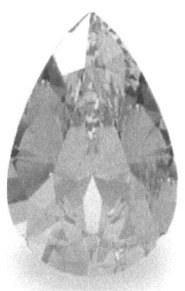

Birth Flowers: Lily of the Valley and Hawthorn.

Lily of the Valley   Common Hawthorn

The month of May, by Simon Bening

May Events

Honorary Months

Presidents, Congresses, and nations around the world issue proclamations recognizing particular months to honor certain causes. These events generally fall in April. (All US unless otherwise noted.)

- American Bike Month
- Asian Pacific American Heritage Month
- Asparagus Month
- Drinking Water Month
- Jewish American Heritage Month
- Mental Heath Awareness Month
- Music Month (New Zealand)
- National ALS Awareness Month
- National Brain Tumor Awareness Month
- National Military Appreciation Month
- National Moving Month
- National Smile Month (United Kingdom)
- Older Americans Month
- Skin Cancer Awareness Month
- South Asian Heritage Month

Moveable and Multi-Day Events

Some events take place over a specific week or time period. Start and finish dates may vary from year to year. Some events occur on different days each year (such as "fourth Saturday of a month").

Victoria Day (Canada)

Victoria Day, a Canadian public holiday in honor of the birthday of Queen Victoria, is celebrated on the last Monday before May 25, meaning that it can occur as early as May 18 and as late as May 24, her actual birthday. It marks the unofficial beginning of summer in Canada. The province of Quebec celebrates *Journée nationale des patriotes* (National Patriots' Day) on the same date.

Vesākha (वैशाख)

The Buddhist holiday day known as Vesākha or simply Vesak commemorates the birth, enlightenment, and death of Gautama Buddha. It is celebrated on the first full moon of the month of Vesākha, which normally falls in April or May, and in leap years in the month of June.

May Zodiac Signs

From the perspective of someone on Earth, the Sun appears to move through the sky throughout the year, along a path astronomers call the ecliptic plane. The ecliptic plane is divided into twelve constellations, known as the zodiac, based on traditionally observed patterns of stars. On your birthday, you can't see your constellation, because it's part of the daytime sky.

The zodiac was first developed by Babylonian astronomers about 2,500 years ago. Because they were unaware that the Earth wobbles like a spinning top (a motion known as *precession*), they didn't make allowance for the fact that the Sun's path through the zodiac changes over time.

That means there are now two sets of dates for your birth sign. The *tropical* dates are the original Babylonian dates; the *siderial* dates tell you where the Sun actually appears as it moves along its annual path.

In tropical reckoning, May 24 is in Gemini, and in siderial reckoning, May 24 is in Taurus.

Gemini

Tropical May 22 to June 21

Siderial June 16 to July 15

In Greek and Roman mythology, Castor and Pollux were twin brothers, both born to Leda. Castor, however, was a mortal, son of the King of Sparta, whereas Pollux was the son of Zeus, who had seduced (or raped) Leda while disguised as a swan. When Castor was killed, Pollux asked to share his divine immortality with his brother, and so Zeus transformed them both into the constellation of Gemini.

In astrology, Gemini is considered a masculine and air sign, ruled by Mercury. Geminis are supposed to be flexible, responsive, and sociable. Positive traits include intelligence and independence; negative traits include impatience and impulsiveness.

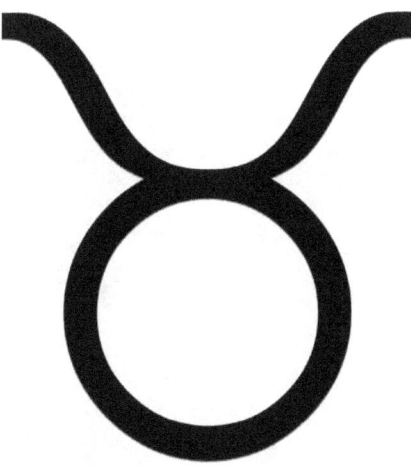

Taurus

Tropical April 21 to May 21

Siderial May 16 to June 15

In Greek mythology, Taurus was a disguise adopted by Zeus, who appeared to the maiden Europa in the form of a gentle white bull. Europa unwisely got too close, and Zeus kidnapped her to the island of Crete, where she bore him three sons, including Minos, builder of the labyrinth that housed the minotaur.

In astrology, Taurus is an earth sign, and Taureans are supposed to be quiet, gentle, compassionate, and stubborn. Taureans can appreciate the finer things in life and are cautious with money.

Illustration by Edward Penfield

What Day of the Week is May 24?

On what day of the week does May 24 fall?

Surprisingly, this isn't an easy question. Because the calendar year is 365 days long (366 in leap years), it doesn't divide evenly by the seven days of the week.

Also, the Earth goes around the Sun in about 365-1/4 days, so a calendar tends to drift over time. That's why the same date falls on different weekdays in different years.

This is made even more complicated by a change in calendars that took place in 1582. Our modern calendar has its roots in ancient Rome, in a calendar reform conducted by Julius Caesar. Caesar commissioned mathematicians to attack the problem, and they came up with the idea of *leap years,* and thus standardized the calendar for centuries to come. This was called the *Julian calendar.*

Over time, however, the small errors in Caesar's calculation compounded. That's why Pope Gregory XIII commissioned the *Gregorian calendar,* used in most of the world today. Some countries converted in 1582, when the calendar was first developed; some converted later; other still haven't changed.

Gregorian and Julian aren't the only types of calendars. The Hebrew year, the Islamic year, and many other calendars are used in different parts of the world and among different people.

You can convert Gregorian dates to other calendars, including the Hebrew calendar, the Islamic calendar, and even the Mayan calendar by visiting the Fourmilab Calendar Converter at http://www.fourmilab.ch/documents/calendar/.

Chinese calendar systems are quite complex and have changed several times; a full discussion is far beyond the scope of this book. If you're interested, you can find information here: http://www.hermetic.ch/cal_stud/chinese_cal.htm.

A 50-year brass perpetual calendar.

Copyright, Credit, and Contact

Follow Us

Our blog *Dobson's Improbable History* (http://improbhistory.blogspot.com) features short articles on events and people associated with each day, and updates several times each week. You can also get a daily "What Happened In History" message and all the latest Timespinner Press news by following us on Facebook at https://www.facebook.com/TimespinnerPress. Our Twitter feed @SidewiseThinker links you to all our News of the Day.

Contact Us

Find an error or a format problem? Want information about the series, about us, or about when the volume for your special day might be available? Please email us at editor@timespinnerpress.com. (We also take requests.)

On Dates

Historians use "CE" (Common Era) and "BCE" (Before the Common Era) instead of the more common "AD" (*Anno Domini*, or Year of Our Lord) and "BC" (Before Christ), reflecting the fact that the year-numbering system established by the Gregorian calendar is used throughout the world in many countries not culturally Christian.

The CE/BCE designation dates back to at least 1708, and have been adopted as a standard by the United Nations and the Universal Postal Union. Because this series of books covers events and people of all nations and cultures, we use the CE/BCE terms.

The abbreviation "O.S." on some dates refers to the fact that the Russian Empire did not switch from the Julian to the Gregorian calendar at the same time as the rest of Europe, and therefore some figures and events have two dates. (See "What Day of the Week…" for an explanation of Julian and Gregorian dates.)

People and events whose original names are not in the Western alphabet have their native names (where possible) in the appropriate script shown in parenthesis. If you are using an e-reader to access an electronic version of this book, all characters don't always display on all devices.

Sources and Art Credits

We owe a great debt to Wikipedia, which is our first stop for research. We attempt to make independent confirmation of all important dates and facts through a variety of other sources. Other sources we frequently use include the Library of Congress; "on this day" listings from *Encyclopedia Britannica*, the New York *Times*, and the BBC; and, of course, the always essential Google.

All art and photographs are either in the public domain, used under a Creative Commons license, or with a "fair use" justification, and most frequently come from Wikimedia Commons and the Library of Congress Prints and Photographs Division.

Attribution is provided where requested by the copyright owner or when of historical significance, listed below. For information about any particular illustration or photograph, please contact us.

- The cover illustration, "The Great East River Suspension Bridge," was created by Currier & Ives in 1892. The interior illustration of the Brooklyn Bridge carries the same title but is from 1883. Both images are in the public domain because their copyrights have expired.

- The illustration of the month of May used on the back cover and as the frontispiece is from the French Gothic illuminated manuscript *Les Très Riches Heures du duc de Berry* by the Limbourg Brothers, Jean Colombe, and an intermediate painter whose name is lost to history. It is in the public domain because its copyright has expired.

- The photograph of the Brooklyn Bridge showing Manhattan in the background was taken by "Hakilon" in 2011. It was dedicated to the public domain by its author under the CC0 1.0 Public Domain Dedication.

- The Russian Orthodox icon of Saints Cyril and Methodius is from the 18th or 19th century. It is in the public domain because its copyright has expired.

- The photograph of the Redstone School was taken in 2007 by Dudesleeper at en.wikipedia, and is used here under the CC BY-SA 3.0 license.

- The 1970 photograph of the Ellicott City railroad station is from the Library of Congress Prints and Photographs Division, Historic American Engineering Record. It was taken by William E. Barrett of the National Park Service and is in the public domain as a work of the US federal government.

- The 1866 photograph of Samuel F. B. Morse was taken by Mathew Brady. It is from the Library of Congress Prints and Photographs Division, Brady-Handy Collection, and is in the public domain because its copyright has expired.

- The photograph of the launch of Aurora 7 is in the public domain as a work of NASA.

- Emanuel Leutze's painting *Washington Crossing the Delaware* can be seen in New York's Metropolitan Museum of Art. This image is from the Google Art Project and is in the public domain because the original work of art is in the public domain.

- The photograph of Reese's Peanut Butter Cups was taken by Evan-Amos for Vanamo Media. It was released into to the public domain under the CC0 1.0 Public Domain Dedication.

- The *Cowboy Bebop* logo is not an object of copyright, but is a trademark. Its noncommercial use simply illustrates a description of its creator.This use does not imply endorsement or ownership of the mark.

- The publicity photograph of Gary Burghoff and McLean Stephenson from *M*A*S*H* is in the public domain because it was published in the United States between 1923 and 1977 without a copyright license.

- The image of Bob Dylan at the 1963 Civil Rights March on Washington is cropped from a larger image showing that he is performing with Joan Baez. The original image is in the collection the National Archives and Records Service and was originally taken by the United States Information Agency. It is in the public domain as a work of the US federal government.

- The portrait photograph of Queen Victoria was taken by Alexander Bassano around 1887. It is in the public domain because its copyright has expired.

- The gold Roman *aureus* with the image of Germanicus was struck around 40 CE during the reign of his son Caligula. The photograph was taken by the Classical Numismatic Group and used here under the CC BY-SA 3.0 license.

- The 1933 photograph of Lionel Conacher playing for the Toronto Crosse and Blackwell Chefs is in the collection of the Canadian Football Hall of Fame. It is in the public domain because its copyright has expired.

- The 1952 photograph of the Lenin Mausoleum is from the Gan-Shmuel archive, and is in the public domain because its copyright has expired. The image has been cropped for its appearance in this book.

- The 1972 publicity photograph of Dan Rowan, Tiny Tim, and Dick Martin from *Rowan & Martin's Laugh-In* is in the public domain because it was published in the United States between 1923 and 1977 without a copyright license. The image has been cropped for its appearance in this book.

- The 1943 photograph of Duke Ellington at the Hurricane Club was taken by Gordon Parks for the Office of War Information, and is now in the collection of the Library of Congress Prints and Photographs Division. It is in the public domain as a work of the US federal government.

- The 1986 photograph of Harold Wilson was taken by Allan Warren and is used here under the CC BY-SA 3.0 license.

- The 1833 painting of abolitionist William Lloyd Garrison by Nathaniel Jocelyn is in the collection of the National Portrait Gallery, Smithsonian Institution. It is in the public domain because its copyright has expired.

- The 18th century portrait of Nicolaus Copernicus by an unknown artist is in the public domain because its copyright has expired. The original is located in the Biblioteka Jagiellońska, Krakow, Poland.

- The photograph of Old and Young Tom Morris was taken betwen 1870 and 1975 by Thomas Rodger. It is in the public domain because its copyright has expired.

- The photograph of an emerald was taken by Les Facettes and is used here under the CC BY-SA 3.0 license.

- The photograph of a lily of the valley (*convallaria majalis*) is by H. Zell and is used here under the CC BY-SA 3.0 license.

- The photograph of a hawthorn (*Crataegus monogyna*) is by Sannse and is used here under the CC BY-SA 3.0 license.

- The illustration of the month of May from *Hennessy Hours* is by Simon Bening, circa 1483/1484 — 1561. It is in the public domain because its copyright has expired.

- The photograph of Czechoslovakian Easter eggs was taken by Jan Kameníček, who has released the image into the public domain.

- The photograph of the 1906 automobile calendar by Edward Penfield is from the Library of Congress Prints and Photographs Division, and is in the public domain because it was published prior to January 1, 1923.

- The 50-year perpetual calendar photograph is in the public domain.

License Description and Terms

Aside from material purely in the public domain, photographs and other material in this book are used under specific licenses permitting free use, usually with attribution. For full text and terms of these licenses, click or enter the appropriate links below.

- Creative Commons Attribution 2.0 Generic (CC BY 2.0): http://creativecommons.org/licenses/by/2.0/deed.en

- Creative Commons Attribution-Share Alike 3.0 Generic (CC BY-SA 3.0): http://creativecommons.org/licenses/by-sa/3.0/

- Creative Commons Attribution-Share Alike 2.5 Generic (CC BY-SA 2.5): http://creativecommons.org/licenses/by-sa/2.5/deed.en

- Creative Commons Attribution-Share Alike 2.0 Generic (CC BY-SA 2.0): http://creativecommons.org/licenses/by/2.0/deed.en http://creativecommons.org/publicdomain/zero/1.0/deed.en

Timespinner
Press